man + dog

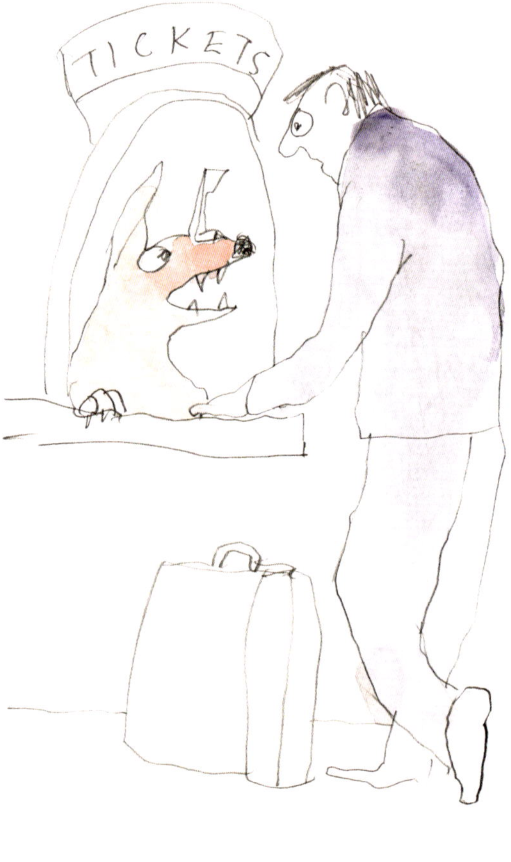
TICKETS

man + dog

drawings by
Nick Wadley

DALKEY ARCHIVE PRESS
CHAMPAIGN / LONDON

Library of Congress Cataloging-in-Publication Data

Wadley, Nicholas.
Man + dog : drawings / by Nick Wadley.
p. cm.
ISBN 978-1-56478-552-7
1. Human beings--Caricatures and cartoons. 2.
Dogs--Caricatures and cartoons. 3. English wit and
humor, Pictorial. I. Title. II. Title: Man and dog. III.
Title: Man plus dog.
NC1479.W33A4 2009
741.5'6942--dc22
2009075242

www.dalkeyarchive.com

Partially funded by a grant from the Illinois Arts
Council, a state agency, and by the University of
Illinois at Urbana-Champaign

Two of these drawings were first published in Nick
Wadley's *The Way It Is* (Wisconsin, Obscure Pub-
lications, 2006); versions of three others first ap-
peared in 2008 on a cd sleeve for Otros Aires, the
Argentine tango band.

Printed on permanent/durable acid-free paper and
bound in Canada

MAN + DOG

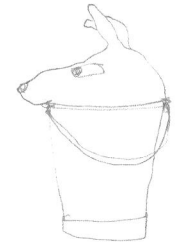

It goes without saying that MAN + DOG = DOG + MAN, as in life.

As importantly, also as in life, MAN + DOG = MAN + MAN.

They hold mirrors to each other—reflecting, comparing and competing. In the end, on balance, DOG appears to have a slight edge? Maybe. But mirrors turn things back-to-front. And, anyway, *through-the-looking-glass* was never the most promising place to look for order,

overtures . . .

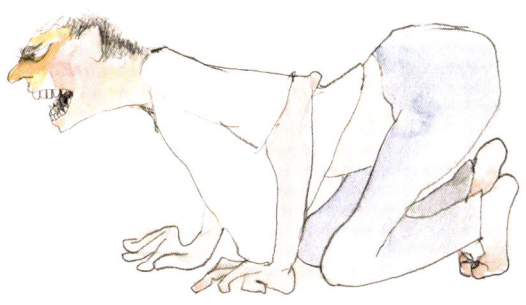

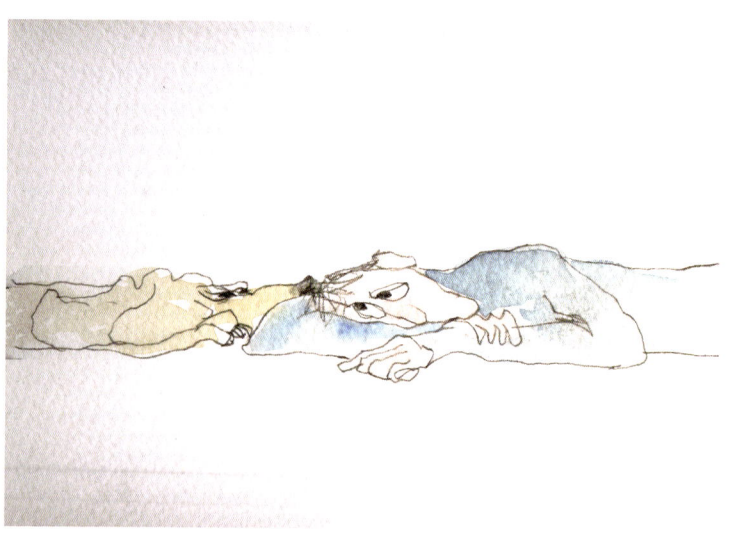

"shall we be frank?"

hair of the dog

dogma

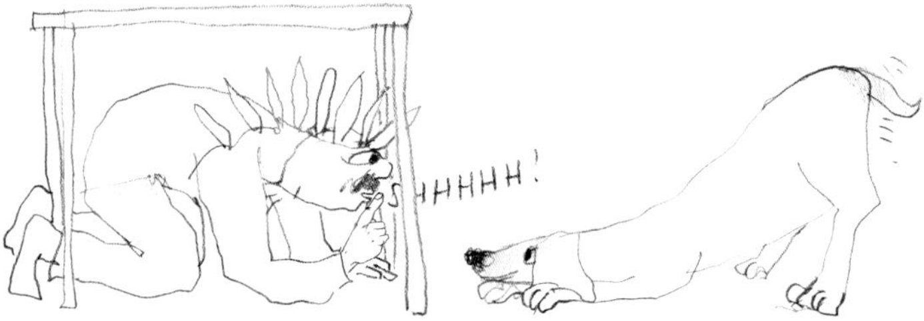
SHHHHHH!

games (indoor)

games (outdoor)

outside of a dog . . .

dog in library

interlude

end of interlude

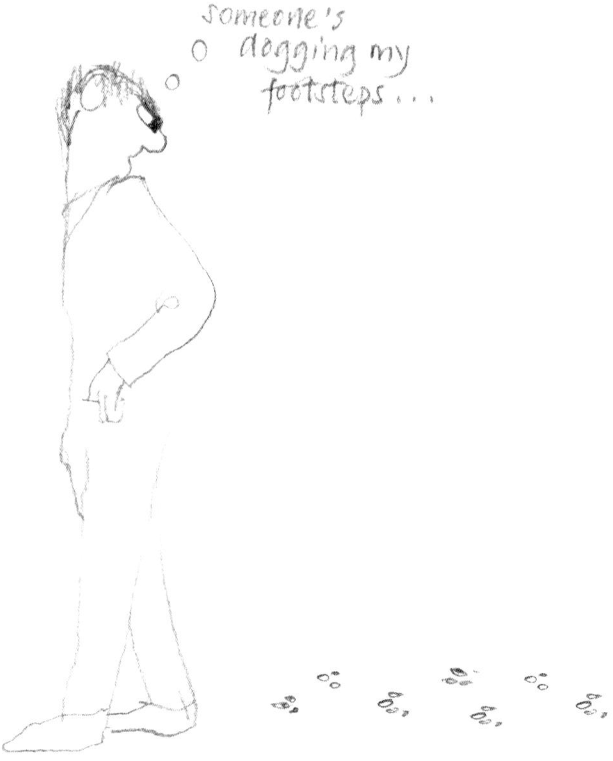
someone's dogging my footsteps...

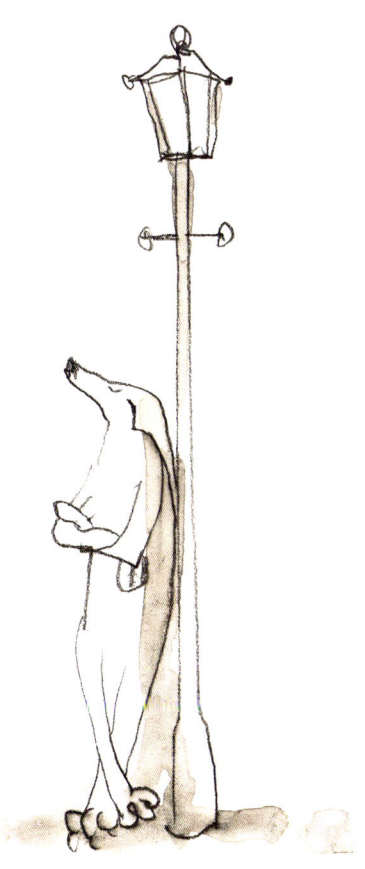

are you DEAF or something?

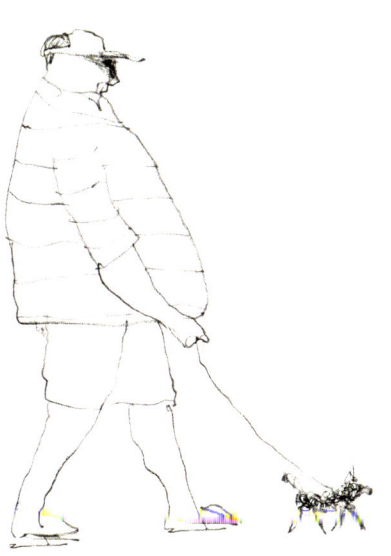

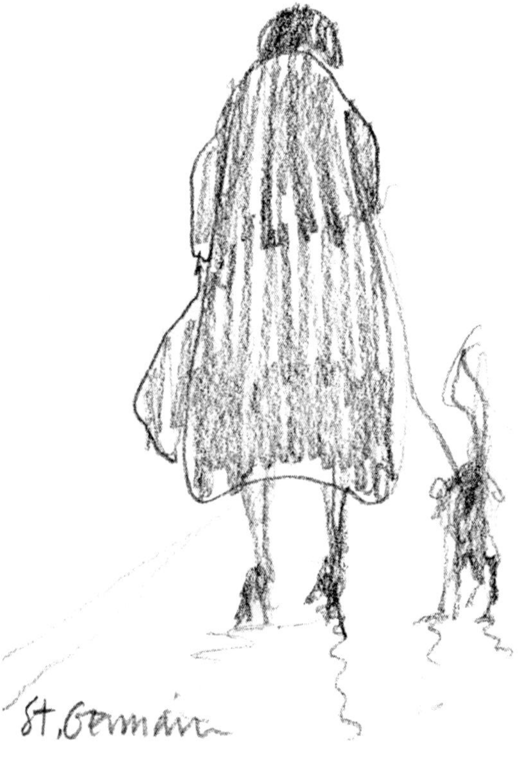
St. Germain

en suite

dog walkers

dog walker

blue ermine

red dog

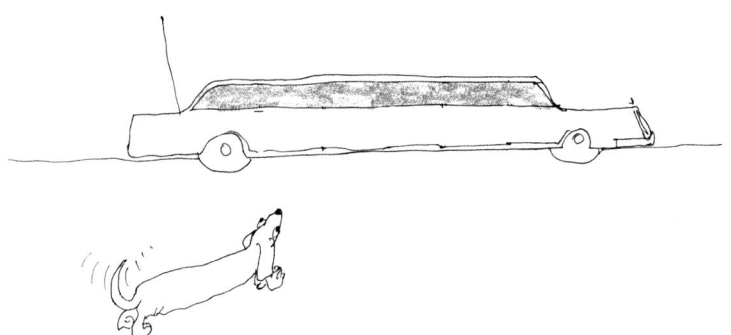

encounter

encounter

it's a wise child . . .

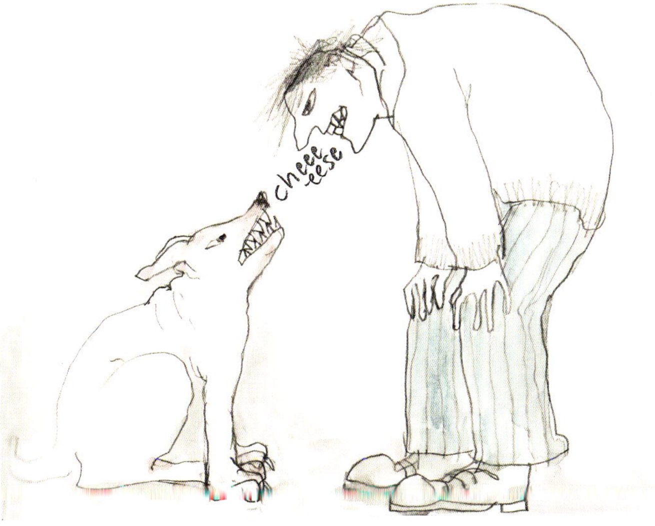
cheeeeese

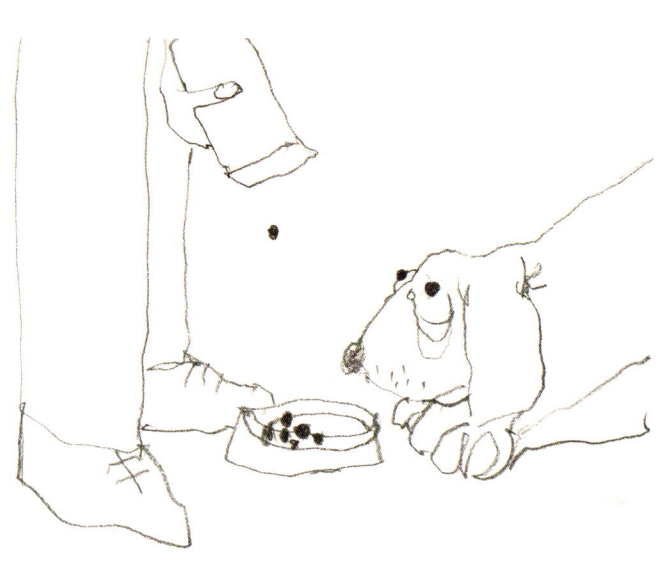

fetch!

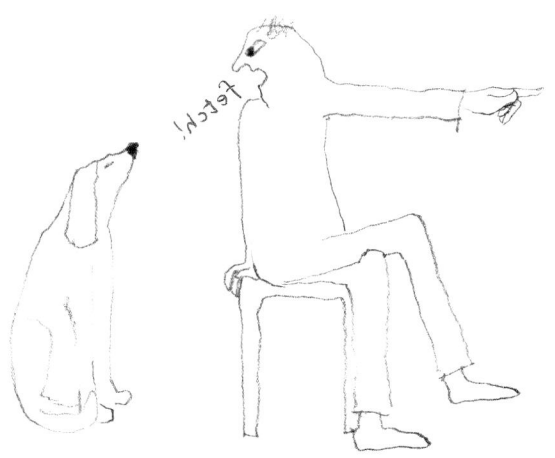

next!

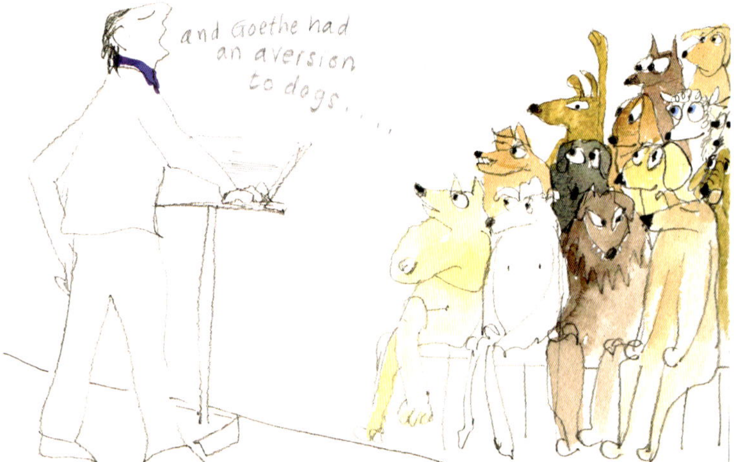
and Goethe had
an aversion
to dogs.....

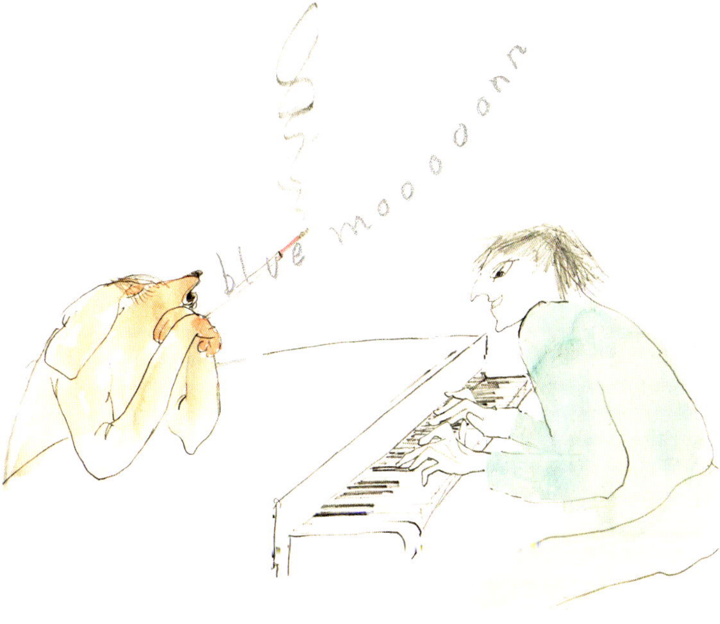
blue mooooon

games (indoor, advanced)

games (outdoor, advanced)

"try to look at it this way—
there's a time for games, and there's now."

POST-SCRIPT

These drawings grew out of a much broader, faintly anthropomorphic family of images made in the 1990s, which were about man and the world at large. Inevitably, a dog found its way into some of them, as dogs do.

And then, around 2001, I made a short series of dog drawings as a birthday book for Jasia Reichardt, in an attempt to defuse her wish to have a real, live, panting dog in the house we share. Some of those drawings have survived here.

While the sequence of images isn't entirely random, the drawings were not conceived as facing pages, and don't pretend to develop a narrative. There is just the timeless, manic *pas de deux*. It's more like a photo album than a storybook. Not all of the pictures have words, and where they do the words usually came later.

A few images were drawn in front of something seen, in the street, like some of the man-walks-dog/dog-walks-man sequence. Some of the rest may have started from around there, but then got filtered down through other routes.

nw

Nick Wadley writes and draws. He taught art history at Chelsea School of Art, London, 1962–1985, and has published on French nineteenth-century painting and drawing. Since the 1990s, he has published several books of cartoons and drawings, and exhibited his drawings in London, Buenos Aires, and Warsaw. He has illustrated works by Robert Walser, U. A. Fanthorpe, Tom Whalen, John Ashbery, Simon Perchik, Lisa Jardine, and others. He was a close friend of Stefan and Franciszka Themerson, and has written about both. He writes occasionally for the *Times Literary Supplement* and other journals.